How to Stay HAPPY

Written by Helen Jaeger

AUTUMN
PUBLISHING

Written by Helen Jaeger
Illustrated by Anne Passchier

Designed by Richard Sykes
Edited by Helen Catt

Copyright © 2021 Igloo Books Ltd

Published in 2021
First published in the UK by Autumn Publishing
An imprint of Igloo Books Ltd
Cottage Farm, NN6 0BJ, UK
Owned by Bonnier Books
Sveavägen 56, Stockholm, Sweden

All rights reserved, including the right of reproduction
in whole or in part in any form.

Manufactured in China. 1021 001
10 9 8 7 6 5 4 3 2 1

Library of Congress Cataloging-in-Publication
Data is available upon request.

ISBN 978-1-83903-668-2
autumnpublishing.co.uk
bonnierbooks.co.uk

Includes **MOOD TRACKER** poster

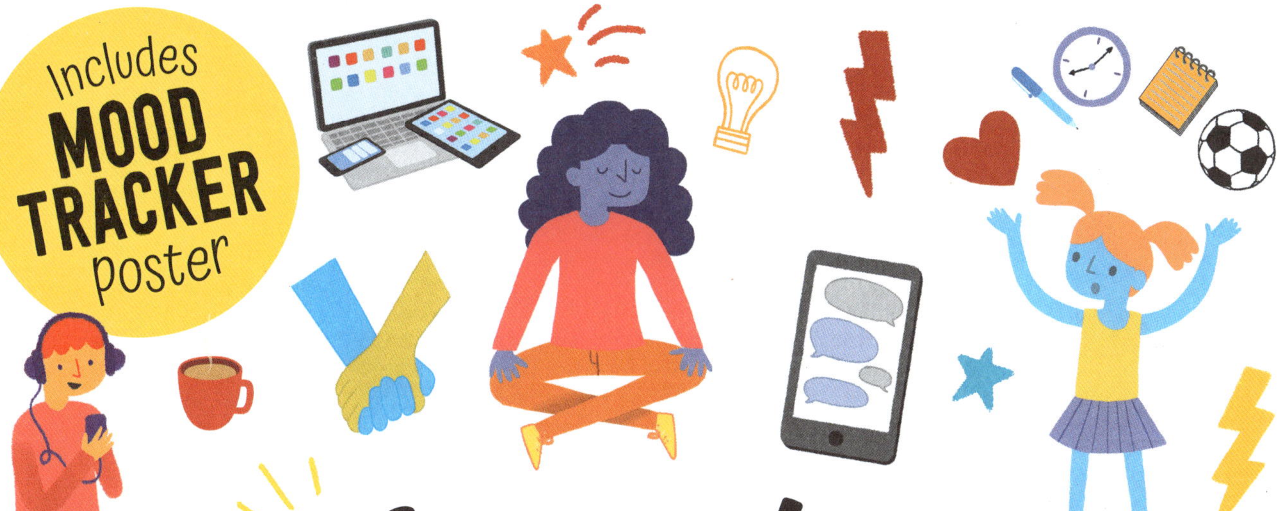

How to STAY HAPPY

Written by Helen Jaeger

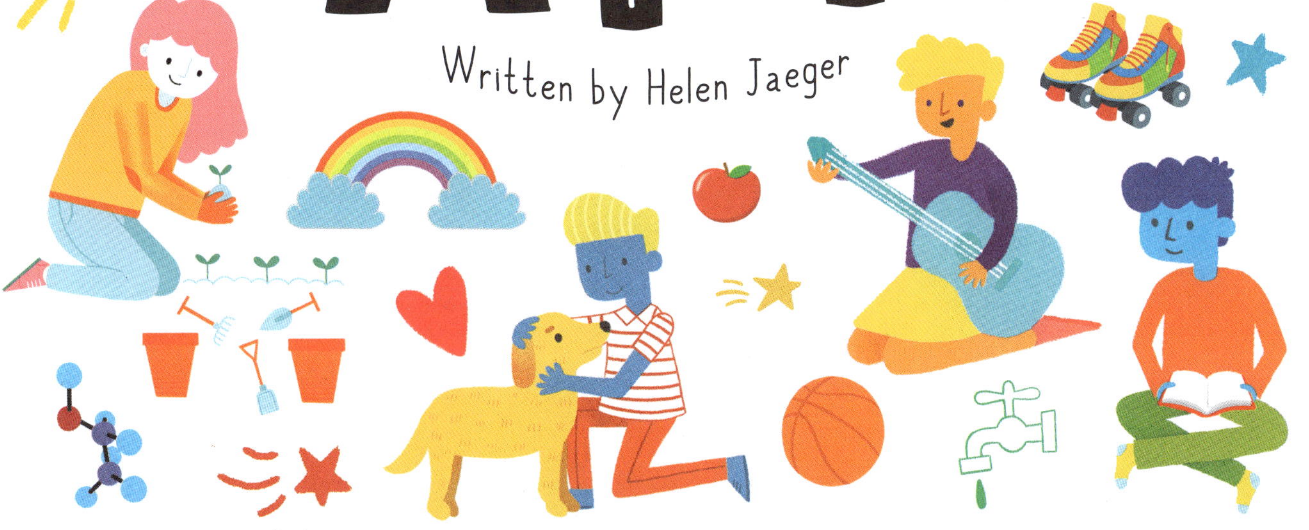

INTRODUCTION

HEY!

Good job for picking up this book! You're about to start an exciting journey to a happy you! There are lots of spaces for you to write and draw. Make this book YOUR OWN! If you ♥ what you see, why not share it with an adult, too?

x

Dear adult,

Welcome to this book about healthy, happy kids. As a Mom and professional children's well-being practitioner, I know how tough the pressures on children are. In this book, you'll find a range of ways for children to get and to stay happy, from how to deal with anger and anxiety to how to deal with serious events, like a death in the family. There are lots of activities children can do by themselves or with you. You could give this book to your child to use as a journal or you could work on ideas together. Whatever you do, I wish you a happy family life!

Helen Jaeger

Contents

I Feel . . .	6
Worry hacker!	8
Emotions game	10
From meh to mad	12
Share your worries	13
How big is your problem?	14
Make a worry monster!	15
Chill out!	16
Stress less	18
Who is important to me?	20
Getting to know you	22
What would a good friend do?	23
Coping with bullying	24
Am I a bully?	26
Affirmations and strengths	27
Ideal me	28
Keep growing	30
I can change	32
Not my circus	33
Anger and my body	34
My anger triggers	35
Coping with anger	36
Boss of my body	38
My safe place	40
Staying safe online	42
Loss	44
Happy helping	46
Help!	48

i FEEL...

What is an emotion? An emotion is a feeling. It's a feeling, because we "feel" it somewhere in our body. Emotions aren't "good" or "bad." They are signals, telling us something about ourselves or the world around us.

Here are some feelings you may know. Next time you have a feeling, **ask yourself, "what is this feeling trying to tell me?"**

Stress
I need to slow down and look after myself.

Happy
Things are going well. I can share that with others.

Sad
I need love and to look for joy.

Worried
I don't know what to do. I can ask for help.

Can you match the emotion to the emoji?

Happy   Disgusted   Confused   Excited   Scared
                Bored   Tired

6

What makes me feel that way?

Look at the emojis and emotions on the opposite page. Choose two of them. Think about a time you felt like that. Who were you with? What were you doing? Draw or write about it in the boxes below.

Feelings come and go. One day we feel happy ("I did well in that test!"), the next sad ("My friend is leaving school!"). A week later we're excited ("It's birthday time!"), then we're tired ("Too many late nights gaming.").

It can be fun to keep a "how did I feel?" diary for a week. Fill in the journal page below with an emoji face for the main emotion you had that day.

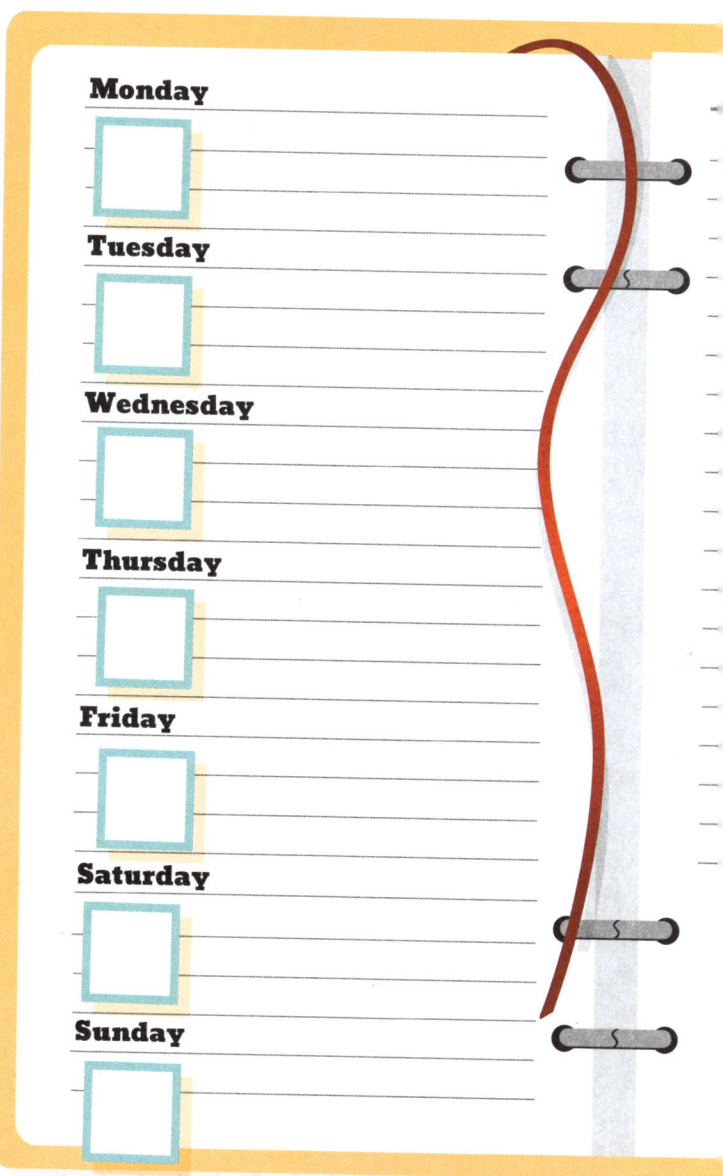

If you find you have lots of feelings like anger, worry, or sadness, talk to an adult you trust about it.

7

WORRY HACKER!

Worries are like monsters: they like the dark, they want us to think they're bigger than they are, and they come in mobs. Use this Worry Hacker to bring each of your worries into the light, where it's much easier to beat them.

I'M WORRIED! → YES / NO

YES → What am I worried about? → Can I do anything about it?
- NO → Think about something good!
- YES! → Make a plan. I can do this...
  - LATER → WHEN? Give a date. → LET YOUR WORRY GO!!
  - NOW → DO IT! → LET YOUR WORRY GO!!

NO → Think about something good!

Take a breath!

Have you noticed we all breathe quicker or hold our breath when we're scared? It's not like when we're doing exercise, where we breathe faster, but deeper.

Taking some slow, deep breaths is a quick way to calm down fast. Here are some fun ways to do it. Try them out!

1. Imagine you're holding a mug of hot chocolate (yum!). Breathe OUT to cool it down and IN to smell it.

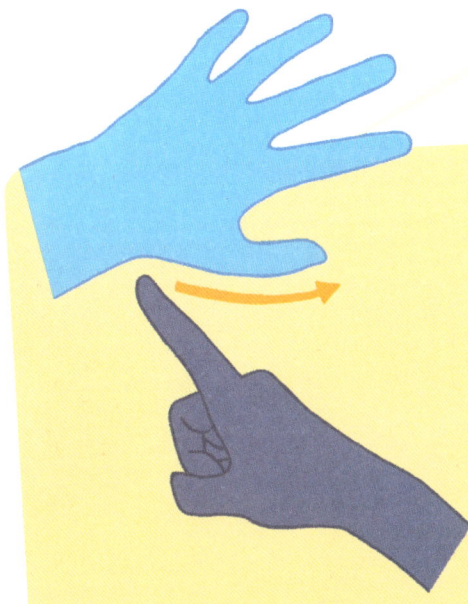

2. Hold up one hand spread out like a starfish. Use your finger from your other hand like a pencil to draw around your hand. Breathe in as you go up each finger, then pause at the top, and breathe out as you slide back down.

3. Blow onto a windmill. How fast can you make it spin and for how long? That long breath out helps you relax.

EMOTIONS GAME

It's good to share feelings with people we trust. Here's a game you can play with another person to share your feelings.

How to play

Use coins or other small objects as tokens. Take turns rolling the dice. Move your token that many times around the board. When you land on a square, it will give you the name of a feeling. Share a time when you felt like this.

START

KEY: Surprised Confused Angry Bored Proud

10

FROM MEH TO MAD

Although you might feel like you go from zero to nuclear when you get mad, the truth is feelings build up in stages. If you can recognize when you start feeling unsettled or irritated, it may help your feelings not to build up. Then you can avoid panicking or getting furious!

Look at the scale for feeling angry and feeling anxiety. Can you remember a time you felt either of these ways? Choose a tip for each step that would help bring down the temperature and make you feel calmer, or come up with one of your own. You might want to use the same tip for more than one level.

ANGER	ANXIETY
Furious	Panicking
Fuming	Stressed
Angry	Anxious
Annoyed	Worried
Irritated	Unsettled
OK	

Tips to help you cope:
- Deep breathing
- Playing with a fidget toy
- Coloring
- Imagining your favorite place
- Stroking a pet
- Talking to someone
- Being active
- Counting back from 10

Write your own ideas here:

Share your worries!

There's an old saying:

"A PROBLEM SHARED IS A PROBLEM HALVED."

"I'm all ears!"

It means it's good to talk. We all need someone to talk to, whether that's a friend, parent, grandparent, or even your pet lizard!

Who can you talk to? Draw around your hand in the space below. In the thumb and fingers, write the names of someone or something* you feel comfortable talking to.

In the middle of the hand, think about who you could talk to if you had a really BIG problem. Maybe it includes a teacher at school or a children's helpline?

* Yes, Foxy the teddy bear, who you got when you were two, counts!

HOW BIG IS YOUR PROBLEM?

It's a fact! Some problems are BIGGER than others! Look at the problems on the right. Where would you put them on the scale of "1, annoying but fixable" to "5, super-emergency, send help now!"

5 HELP! EMERGENCY. You may need to contact emergency services or go to the hospital.

4 HUGE PROBLEM. You may need help from an adult to fix it. Bullying or wanting to hurt yourself would fit here.

3 MEDIUM PROBLEM. It's solvable, but you may have to do something you don't want to do or don't like.

2 SMALL PROBLEM. You can change it with some effort.

1 TINY PROBLEM. You can fix this yourself, easy!

TOP TIP:
One way to be emotionally smart is to match your feeling to your situation. Try not to get uptight about the small stuff. Save that for when you've got a BIG problem.

- [ ] You get blamed for something you didn't do.
- [ ] Someone accidentally bumps into you.
- [ ] You forget to do your homework.
- [ ] Someone calls you names.
- [ ] You're being cyberbullied.
- [ ] Someone hacked your game account.
- [ ] Your friend is worried about a test.
- [ ] Your friend is hurting themselves.
- [ ] You don't like your teacher.
- [ ] You don't win a race.
- [ ] Someone takes your pencil.
- [ ] You want to go outside, but it's raining.
- [ ] You have a stomachache.
- [ ] Someone took your money.
- [ ] You forget your lunch box.
- [ ] You fell over.
- [ ] Mom and Dad argue all the time.

MAKE YOUR OWN WORRY MONSTER

Ever wished you had someone who could magically take your worries away? Well, now you do! Make your very own worry monster to eat all those troubling worries. Here's how.

Trace this template and cut it out. Copy a big toothy mouth at the top and bottom of your monster. Use a ruler to draw some lines in the middle.

Fold along the dotted lines. Decorate the back with a good monster-y pattern. The top section is the monster's face. You can decorate it with eyes and ears.

Now open it up and write what's worrying you on the lines. When you've finished, fold it over again. Your monster has eaten your worries!

WORRIES!

OM NOM NOM!

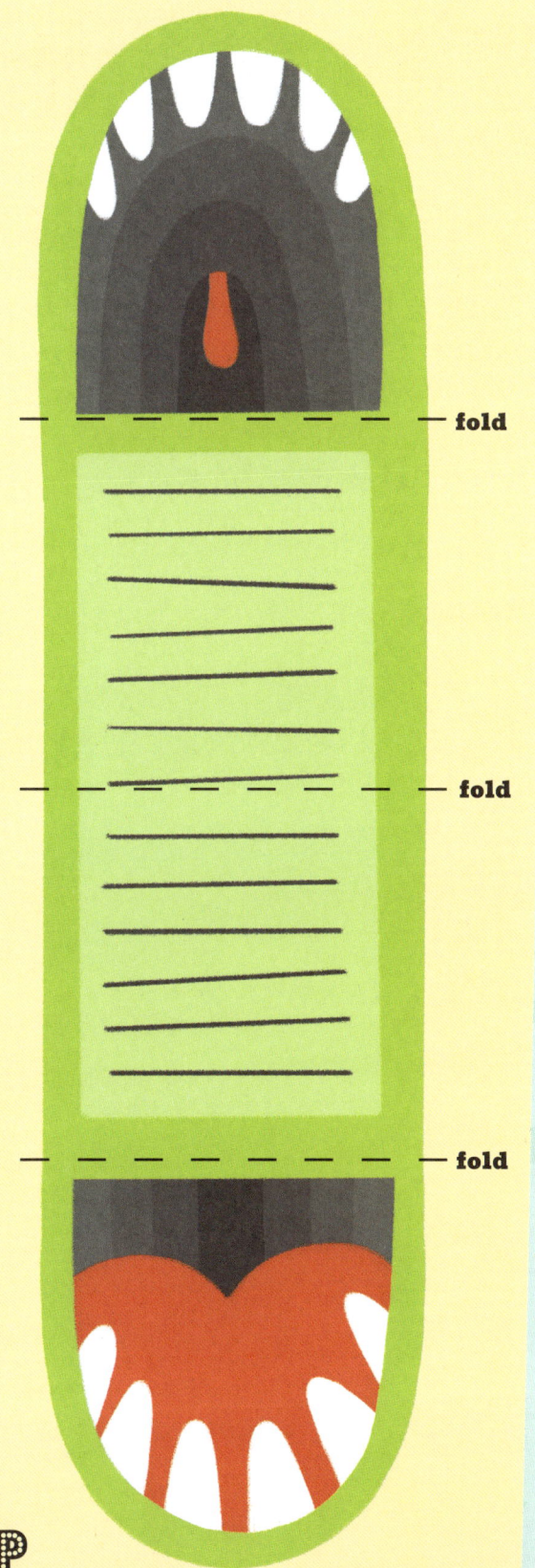

REMEMBER:
YOU CAN ASK FOR HELP

CHILL OUT!

Chilling out makes everyone happier! How good at relaxing are you? Here are three different ways to help you relax.

Be more cat

Ever notice how chilled out they are? They love nothing more than a nap in the sun. Close your eyes and lie in a comfortable position. Imagine you're a cat. You've seen a mouse in your dream! Tense up your arms, shoulders, and hands, as though you're about to pounce. Gradually let them relax. Next imagine you're on a high wall about to jump off. Tense up your feet and legs. Then gradually relax them. Time to stretch. Stretch out your arms and legs as far as you can. You can give a big yawn, too. Doesn't that feel better?

Chilly fingers

Imagine you're holding an ice cube in each of your fists. Really focus on the feeling of cold in each of your fingers, then imagine the cool tingly feeling spreading up your hands, into your arms, and then down your spine, until your whole body feels cool and calm.

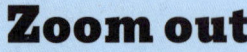

Zoom out

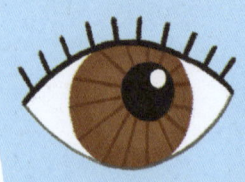

Relax your eyes, too, especially if you have a lot of screen time. Look up from your screen (or whatever you're focusing on). Focus on something near. Then a bit farther away. And then really far away. Then go back the other way until you're focused back where you started.

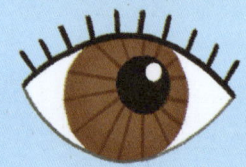

Get some rest!

One of the best ways to be happy is to make sure you get enough sleep! When we sleep, our bodies do amazing things!

Sleep helps you stress less.

Sleep helps you store good memories.

Sleep helps your body repair.

Sleep helps you be creative.

Sleep helps you concentrate better.

Sleep keeps your heart healthy.

Are you getting enough sleep?

If you're aged 6-12 years, you need 9-12 hours sleep. That means if you get up at 7 am, the latest you should be asleep is 10 pm! Use this log to keep check of how much sleep you get.

MON	TUES	WED	THURS	FRI	SAT	SUN
Time to bed:	Time to bed:	Time to bed:	Time to bed:	Time to bed:	Time to bed:	Time to bed:
Hours of sleep:	Hours of sleep:	Hours of sleep:	Hours of sleep:	Hours of sleep:	Hours of sleep:	Hours of sleep:
Enough?	Enough?	Enough?	Enough?	Enough?	Enough?	Enough?

STRESS LESS

Another great way to relax is to use your imagination. When we think of good things, we feel good! This is called meditation. Use the meditation below to help you relax. You could ask your favorite adult to read it out to you. It's about your favorite teddy bear. You could hold your teddy as you do this meditation.

Close your eyes. Imagine you are holding your favorite teddy bear. Notice how soft your bear feels. You give your bear a hug. As you hug your bear, he* comes to life. To your amazement, your bear starts to grow before your eyes! Now he is twice as big as you. You look into his eyes. He is looking at you with so much love and kindness. He opens his big fluffy arms to welcome you into a hug. As he hugs you, you feel happy, warm, and safe. Lean on his big, warm, fluffy tummy. Now your bear wants to hear about any worries or problems you have. As you speak, he listens very carefully. Something magical happens! The more you tell your bear, the better you feel. You feel light and happy and calm. When you finish speaking, he gives you an extra special hug. He tells you he loves you. He says you can always speak to him.

(* or she!)

MAKE A STRESS BALL

Ever noticed that when you feel angry or worried, your body tenses up? It's as if your body is storing up energy ready to fight or run away. It doesn't always feel good. One way to get rid of this extra energy is to use a stress ball. As you squeeze a stress ball, your extra energy drains away, until you're back to feeling relaxed. Phew!

Do this outside or somewhere you can make a mess.

You will need:
- ☑ Balloon
- ☑ Funnel
- ☑ Scissors
- ☑ Marker pens
- ☑ Flour
- ☑ Clothespin

Instructions:

1 Blow into the balloon, until it is about the width of your hand. Pinch the opening shut to keep the air in or use a clothespin, but don't tie it.

2 Carefully insert the funnel in the balloon opening. A little air may escape, but don't worry. Pour the flour inside the funnel to fill the balloon.

3 When it is full, remove the funnel, keeping the balloon top pinched. Gently squeeze out any air that remains and tie the balloon closed. Cut off any extra balloon top, being careful not to puncture the rest of the balloon.

4 Decorate it how you like, maybe with a funny face, your name or patterns. Now you have a stress ball!

WHO IS IMPORTANT TO ME?

One way we feel happy is when we love and are loved by others. That could be your Mom, Dad, brother or sister, cousin, friend, or even your pet cat. Who is important to you? Who makes you happy? Celebrate these special people by drawing them in the frames below.

RECIPE FOR FRIENDSHIP

There's a saying:

"TO HAVE GOOD FRIENDS, BE A GOOD FRIEND."

So what makes a good friend? Have a look at the list of ingredients below. Make up your own recipe for friendship.

Trustworthiness

Fun

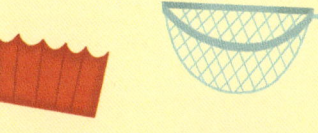
Kindness

Love

Honesty

Understanding

Loyalty

Ingredients

Instructions

GETTING TO KNOW YOU

It can be scary trying to make new friends! What can you talk about? What can you do together? Here are some ideas. Maybe you have some of your own, too?

Things to ask

- Can I play, too?
- What's your name?
- What do you like to do?
- What's your favorite game?
- Who's in your family?
- Do you have a pet?
- What's your favorite book/movie/band?
- What was the best vacation you went on?
- What do you want to get on your birthday?
- Where would you go if you could go anywhere?

Things to do

- Invite someone to play a game with you.
- Invite someone to your house for a playdate (ask an adult first).
- Go for a bike ride together.
- Help each other with homework.
- Play online games together.
- Pick someone to be your partner in class or PE.
- Learn some jokes and share them.
- Go bug-hunting together.
- Go swimming together.
- Do art together.
- Share things with your new friend.

More ideas:

22

WWAGFD?
(What Would A Good Friend Do?)

Have a look at the questions below. WWAGFD? Circle your answers. What kind of friend are YOU?

1 Your friend falls over in the playground. Do you:

a) Ignore him? You're having fun playing your own game.

b) Laugh at him? It was so funny the way he fell over!

c) Run over and ask him if he's hurt?

2 Your Mom has said you can have a friend over. You have to choose between your two best friends. Do you:

a) Tell both at the same time and say "tough luck" to the one you didn't choose?

b) Tell one and keep it a secret?

c) Tell the one you didn't choose that you're really sorry, Mom said only one person could come and you'd love for them to come next time.

3 Your friend wants to join your online game, but you're winning and you don't want her to join, because she's better than you. Do you:

a) Tell her she's not welcome?

b) Tell her there's a glitch and she can't join?

c) Decide friendship is more important and say, Yeah, of course, that'd be great!

4 A popular kid from another class says your friend is ugly. Do you:

a) Laugh and agree with them?

b) Get annoyed but say nothing?

c) Disagree with the popular kid and say your friend is great!

How did you do?

Mostly a:
Maybe put yourself in the other person's shoes and think how you'd feel. Being caring is part of being a good friend.

Mostly b:
It's important that our friends know we have their back. Remember, loyalty is really important in friendships!

Mostly c:
Can we be friends? You rock at it!

COPING WITH BULLYING

Experts reckon 1 in 4 of us experiences bullying at some time or another. It could be obvious, like someone hitting or pinching you. Or hidden, like nasty gossip. Here are some ways you can beat the bully.

1. DON'T REACT. Although it can be tough, try not to show the bully how much they hurt you, and try not to do the same things back. When things start to spiral, they get harder to deal with.

2. CALMLY ASK THEM TO STOP. Say "that's not funny" or "stop bugging me." Sometimes people do things that are unkind or hurtful by accident or without thinking. If this is the case, then talking to them may help fix things.

3. REMEMBER YOUR WORTH. Bullying always says more about the bully than about the person being bullied. You never deserve to be bullied, and it's not your fault. Never forget your own inner strength, worth, and talents.

4. AVOID THEM. It's okay to avoid situations when you're alone with the bully, as long as you talk to a grown-up to explain why you're doing it. You shouldn't give up doing things you enjoy because of a bully, but if it's helpful to take a short break while things settle, you can.

5. DON'T JOIN IN. Don't join in making jokes about yourself. You can't control what a bully says about you, but you don't need to let it change what you say about yourself.

6. TELL SOMEONE. You are not alone in this, and it's not up to you to stop bullying by yourself. Talk to someone who can help, like your parents or teacher.

7. SPEND TIME WITH PEOPLE WHO LOVE YOU. Bullying is hurtful, and it can make it hard to remember the good things about yourself. Spend time with your friends and family who make you feel good about yourself. You can talk to them about how you feel or just do something fun to help you feel better.

SAY NO TO BULLYING

If someone else is being bullied, don't join in. Tell someone. You might want to make an extra special effort to be kind to the person being bullied. Include them in your conversations or invite them to play with you.

AM I BEING BULLIED?

Sometimes it's hard to know if you're being bullied. People can knock into you accidentally. Or borrow your pencil without asking. They might make a joke that they think is funny, without realizing it's hurt your feelings. Usually they'd quickly say sorry, if asked.

Bullies MEAN what they do (that's why they're MEANIES). They often do it over a long time. This guide can help you know if you're being bullied. There are lots of different ways that bullying can look, though, so if you're ever unsure, speak to someone.

- Do other people laugh at you?
  a) never b) sometimes c) often

- Do others imitate the way you walk, talk, or dress?
  a) never b) sometimes c) often

- Do you feel alone at school or other places?
  a) never b) sometimes c) often

- Has someone told your secrets or spread lies about you?
  a) never b) sometimes c) often

- Are you ever afraid to go to school or activities?
  a) never b) sometimes c) often

- Does someone physically hurt you?
  a) never b) sometimes c) often

- Does someone damage your things?
  a) never b) sometimes c) often

- Do other people say nasty things about you online?
  a) never b) sometimes c) often

- Is someone making you feel anxious or depressed?
  a) never b) sometimes c) often

If you answered:

Mostly a:
Phew, you're not being bullied! Make sure people around you aren't as well.

Mostly b:
Can you tell the person or people involved how you feel? If they say sorry and stop, they didn't mean it.

Mostly c:
Sounds like you're being bullied. Don't put up with it. Get some help NOW.

 # AM I A BULLY?

It's not always easy to spot if you're a bully. Most people would be horrified to think they were. But it's worth checking whether you do any of the following. If in doubt, ALWAYS BE KIND.

I make people upset on purpose.
☐ Never ☐ Sometimes ☐ Often

I like annoying people.
☐ Never ☐ Sometimes ☐ Often

I don't care what someone else thinks or feels.
☐ Never ☐ Sometimes ☐ Often

When I get aggressive, I feel good.
☐ Never ☐ Sometimes ☐ Often

I like making people cry.
☐ Never ☐ Sometimes ☐ Often

I split up people's friendships.
☐ Never ☐ Sometimes ☐ Often

I like being in control of others.
☐ Never ☐ Sometimes ☐ Often

Being sarcastic about someone is fun.
☐ Never ☐ Sometimes ☐ Often

I feel powerful when I share people's secrets.
☐ Never ☐ Sometimes ☐ Often

I give people wrong information on purpose.
☐ Never ☐ Sometimes ☐ Often

I like it when other people laugh at someone.
☐ Never ☐ Sometimes ☐ Often

If you answered "often" to any of these questions, then it's time to have a big think about what you're doing and why.

If you think you might be bullying someone:

STOP
Stop what you're doing and TALK to a grown-up. Even if you're scared about getting into trouble, the most important thing is to get help before things get worse.

THINK
Is there something else in your life that's upsetting you and making you want to lash out? There is never an excuse for taking out bad feelings on other people, but knowing why you're feeling upset is a good way to start changing your behaviour.

MAKE IT RIGHT
Say sorry to the person, or people, you've hurt. You can do this in person or by a letter or text if that's too tricky. If you've been leaving someone out, make an effort to include them. If you've been saying mean things behind their back, make an effort to say kind things, and stop other people if you hear them saying mean things.

STICK WITH IT
Saying sorry only means something if you stop doing the hurtful things. Talk to a grown-up if you're finding it difficult, and keep trying to be kind every day.

AFFIRMATIONS AND STRENGTHS

One way we can change our feelings is by what we say to ourselves.

Say to yourself: I am worthless, lazy, and stupid. How did it make you feel? Probably bad! Now try this. Say to yourself: I am talented, loved, and unique. How did that make you feel? Hopefully better.

We need to treat ourselves like our best friend would, by saying positive things to ourselves. These are called affirmations. Here are some affirmations you could use. Try them now!

- I am a good person.
- I am safe.
- I do my best.
- I am creative.
- I am helpful.
- I can change the world.
- I am enough.
- I am worthy of respect.
- I am important.
- I am loved.
- I welcome challenges.

Which ones are your favorites? Can you think of any of your own?

Ideal Me

One way we feel happy is when we're living our best lives. This is called our ideal self. It's ideal, because it's exactly what we want. It's different for different people. Your friend might want to be an Olympic swimmer, but you hate the pool. Or you might want to be an author, but your brother can't stand English class.

Think about yourself in ten years' time. What do you look like? What will you be doing? What will be important to you? Draw or write what you think below.

Think about ways you could begin to make that now. If you love swimming, are you part of a club? If you want to be an artist, are you drawing regularly? Taking steps now is part of what will make you happy.

One step I can take now is to:

MY SHIELD

Everyone is unique. Your sister likes pasta, but you hate it. You love animals, but your Mom is allergic to dogs. It's okay to be different. The world would be boring if we were all the same! Likewise, we all have different strengths, goals, and wishes.

Celebrate who YOU are. Fill in the shield below with what makes you YOU!

1. Draw a picture of yourself here.

2. MY STRENGTHS. What are you good at?

3. MY GOALS. What do you want to achieve?

4. MY WISHES. If a genie could grant you a wish, what would it be?

KEEP GROWING

Do you remember the time you learned how to brush your teeth or get yourself dressed? Or, later, when you figured out how to cross the street or ride a bike? We're not born knowing this stuff. We have to learn it. But imagine if you'd said: "I can't ride a bike" or "I'll never learn to brush my teeth." Now you'd be really stuck!

We all get stuck, sometimes, when we're learning something new. Maybe you're tempted to give up? Or you say to yourself "it's just too hard." But you don't often give up, right? Experts call this ability to keep trying a **growth mindset**. It's about encouraging yourself, when the going gets tough.

Instead of telling yourself negative things, like, "I'll never be good at this," try something kinder. Here are some sentences that might help.

- I can't do it ... yet.
- Getting better takes time.
- Making mistakes is smart. It's how we learn.
- I can try hard things.
- I don't have to get it 100% right.
- It's OK not to know.

Choose your favorite and, next time you get stuck, keep repeating it until you succeed!

GROW!

I CAN'T BE BOTHERED!

Ever have the blahs, the mehs, the "can't be bothered"s? We all do, from time to time. The problem is, if you don't sometimes push yourself, you won't get stuff done, whether that's finishing your math homework or building an awesome model rocket!

When we feel this way it's like we've lost our get-up-and-go-ness. We don't feel **motivated**.

SCIENCE BIT

Experts say there are two types of motivation. One is **INtrinsic**: it comes from inside ourselves. The other is **EXtrinsic**: it comes from outside ourselves. So, with the pesky homework, you might say to yourself: "I must get it done, because I want to get good grades" (intrinsic) or "I must get it done, because if I don't, my teacher will keep me in at recess" (extrinsic).

You may have heard a saying about using the "carrot or the stick" on a stubborn animal, like a donkey. In this case, your willpower is the donkey (sorry!). A stick is something the donkey wants to run away from. And a carrot is a tempting treat the donkey runs toward. Guess which the donkey prefers? Of course, the carrot.

Like our donkey, we feel more motivated when we know there's a reward in sight. So a good way to motivate yourself is by using a reward chart. Figure out what you need to change and what the reward will be, like a movie night, extra game time, or another treat (maybe agree it with your adult). Give yourself a checkmark every day you achieve, until you reach your target.

I will:						
MON	TUES	WED	THURS	FRI	SAT	SUN

My reward is:

31

i CAN CHANGE

Sometimes we get into bad habits that are difficult to change (gaming after bedtime, anyone??). However much we use a reward chart, our bad habits can still trip us up. When this happens, we need to go on a mission to make ourselves believe we can, and want, to change.

Here are your MM* (Mission Motivation) instructions...

Name your bad habit:

	Tell yourself	Do this
Step 1	I NEED TO CHANGE THIS!	Work out reasons why you really, really need to break your bad habit. And what will happen if you don't.
Step 2	I WANT TO CHANGE THIS!	Tell yourself you really want this change.
Step 3	I'M FIGURING OUT HOW!	Go online, talk to friends/adults, and figure out how to make that change.
Step 4	I'M DOING IT!	Draw up a reward chart or a way of recording your progress.
Step 5	I'M KEEPING GOING...	You may slip up, but you're making great progress. Think about a reward.

Here's an example for late-night, no-sleep gamers!

Bad habit: Gaming late

	Tell yourself	Do this
Step 1	I NEED TO CHANGE THIS!	I'm always tired and grumpy at school. I'm beginning to fight with friends and get into trouble.
Step 2	I WANT TO CHANGE THIS!	I'm sick of waking up feeling tired. I'll end up failing my work and losing my friends.
Step 3	I'M FIGURING OUT HOW!	OK, I will leave all my gaming stuff out of my bedroom or turn it off at bedtime. I'll give my phone to Mom or Dad, too, so I'm not tempted to use it.
Step 4	I'M DOING IT!	Wow! I've done three nights and already I feel better. I have waaaay more energy and had fun playing football at lunch.
Step 5	I'M KEEPING GOING...	It's been three weeks and, with some slipups, I've kept my gaming before bedtime. I sleep well and wake up recharged. I'm even joining a football team!

32

NOT MY CIRCUS, NOT MY MONKEYS!

Sometimes, when we try to make changes, we worry about things we don't have any control over. That can be really stressful!! We need to make sure we're only focusing on what we are responsible for, not what someone else is responsible for.

Think about the things you worry about. Ask yourself: am I responsible for this or not? For example, you ARE responsible for doing your homework, but you're NOT responsible for your Mom's boss making her upset (adults have to figure out stuff, too!).

Look at the circuses above. Imagine you own the blue monkeys. Write down things you're responsible for in the boxes near them. Now think of some things that you are NOT responsible for. Write them near the orange monkeys. You don't have to worry about the orange monkeys. That's someone else's problem!

Top tip: If you're not responsible for something, you don't have to worry about changing it!

ANGER AND MY BODY

Think back to a time when you were angry. What did you feel in your body?

Maybe your fists clenched, your heart started racing, or you felt dizzy or had a headache. Or perhaps you wanted to shout, scream, cry, or hit someone or something. Anger is a powerful feeling!

Anger feels different to everyone. Mark on the body all the places YOU feel your anger. What does it feel like?

What does anger feel like to you?

Anger can feel like...

- Pricking pins
- Red-hot flames
- Icy cold
- Something all scrunched up
- Zaps of lightning

34

MY ANGER TRIGGERS

We all feel angry from time to time, but what bothers your friend may not bother you at all. And what makes you mad may make them say "meh." We're all different. Handling anger means knowing what kicks you off.

Have a look at the triggers below. Sort them into:

A Makes me annoyed

B Makes me angry

C Makes me furious

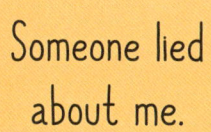

- My teacher scolded me.
- Someone sat in my seat. 
- Someone is being mean to my friend.
- Someone lied about me.
- Everyone laughed at me. 
- I spilled my drink on my homework.
- Someone threw a ball at me.
- My friends weren't playing the game right.
- Someone pushed in line.
- My sister ignores me.

Do you spot any patterns? For example, do you get extra mad when things are unfair, or when someone is deliberately mean?

35

COPING WITH ANGER

Luckily, there are lots of ways you can help yourself calm down when you're feeling angry. Just like the triggers on the previous page, what works for someone else may not work for you. Try these ideas out next time you can feel yourself getting angry and see which ones work for YOU.

- Take three deep breaths.
- Imagine the person who's annoying you wearing silly clothes.
- Talk to someone about your feelings.
- Hit a pillow or cushion (safely).
- Relax your muscles from your toes to the top of your head.
- Count back from 10.
- Go for a walk.
- Think of a place that makes you happy.
- Do your favorite sport.

Can you think of any more? Write them here:

CALMING DOWN

Think about which of the coping skills on the previous page work best for you. Choose five and write them on the petals of the flower below.

COPING SKILLS

BOSS OF MY BODY

Our bodies are amazing! We can run, jump, sing, hug, play sports, and do all sorts of things. As we grow up, it's important to remember that YOU are the boss of your body. No one has a right to do something with it that you don't like.

Here are three rules for making sure YOU are the Boss of your Body!

1 YOU CAN SAY NO. You have a right to say "no" if you don't want your body to be touched. You don't have to hug, kiss, or be touched, if you don't want to.

2 YOU DON'T HAVE TO KEEP SECRETS. No one should make you feel embarrassed or humiliated about your body. You shouldn't be asked to "keep secrets" about your body. Tell someone if this happens.

3 YOU CAN ALWAYS TELL. If someone makes you feel sad, scared, or nervous by the way they treat your body, it's important to tell someone. You won't get in trouble, and it's never too late to tell, even if it's something that happened a while ago.

If there's no one you feel comfortable talking to in person, or if you want some extra help, there are lots of resources at the back of this book.

Can you think of three people you trust who you could talk to if you need to? Write their names here.

1.
2.
3.

SAFE & UNSAFE TOUCH

There are times when it's okay for someone to touch our bodies. Like when Mom wants to give you a hug to show she loves you. Or the nurse needs to look at your knee when you fell over.

Safe touch can also be divided into wanted or unwanted touch. Your answers for what is wanted or unwanted might be completely different than your friend's.

Check out these situations. Then decide: safe, unsafe, or unwanted touch?

Remember: Just as you can politely say "no" to unwanted touch, other people might sometimes want to say no to you. It's important to be respectful.

- A dentist asks to look in your mouth.
- A doctor wants to touch your leg, where there's a cut.
- An aunt you don't like gives you a hug.
- Someone hits you.
- Your classmate nudges you to get your attention.
- Someone wants you to photo your private parts.
- Your brother wants a tickle fight, but you don't.
- Your friend hugs you.
- Your favorite uncle pats you on the head.
- Someone pinches you.

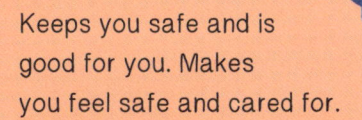

SAFE TOUCH
Keeps you safe and is good for you. Makes you feel safe and cared for.

THESE ARE OK!

UNSAFE TOUCH
Hurts your or other people's bodies or feelings.

THESE ARE NOT OK!

UNWANTED TOUCH
Safe, but you don't want them at the moment.

IT'S OK TO POLITELY SAY NO!

MY SAFE PLACE

Where is your safe place? This is the place you feel relaxed and happy. Maybe it's on your bed with your cat? Or walking along your favorite beach with your family? Take some time to draw and write about your safe place here. It can be real or imaginary.

If you ever start to feel stressed or worried, remembering your safe place can help you to stay calm!

What can you see? _____
What can you smell? _____
What can you taste? _____
What can you hear? _____
What can you touch? _____
Anything else? _____

THREE ISLANDS

Here's a fun activity to help you sort out all the things that make you happy from the things you want to avoid. Imagine three different islands and follow the instructions. Do you notice any patterns with what you put on each island?

THE RED ISLAND This is where you don't want to be. Draw people, places, and objects that you don't want to be part of your life here.

THE ORANGE ISLAND This is where you want to be sometimes. Draw people, places, or things on this island that you sometimes want. You can visit the orange island sometimes and you can also have visitors from orange island.

THE GREEN ISLAND This is where you want to be. Draw your favorite people, places, or things on this island.

41

STAYING SAFE ONLINE

The internet can be a great place to have fun. But what happens when cyberbullies, trolls, and hackers get into your accounts? They can make your online space not only frustrating, but also scary and dangerous.

BE PROTECTED

The best way to make sure you stay safe online is to protect yourself. Think about these things happening in real life:

> A masked stranger asks to be your friend.

> A person your family has never heard of wants to hang out with you.

> Someone offers you presents if you'll play with them.

> Someone you don't know asks for your or your friends' personal details, like name, address, age, and school.

What would YOU do? Chances are, you'd say NO!

Online life is no different. Unless you are totally sure the person you are talking with is who they say they are,

BE CAREFUL!

BE PREPARED

The internet is a great place to find games, chat with friends, get creative, and explore the world. But sometimes you come across something scary or upsetting.

Another way online life can be upsetting is if you or your friend gets bullied. Cyberbullies are hard to beat, as you often don't know much about them. The best way to beat cyberbullies is to be PREPARED.

If anything on the internet upsets you:

1. Talk to someone you trust. They can help you with your worries and sort it out with you.

2. If you don't have an adult to talk to, try a helpline for your state.

3. Decide if what you've seen needs reporting, for example if someone is being hurt. Most websites will have instructions on how to report harmful content, but you can always ask someone to help you.

Most important of all, **DON'T BOTTLE IT UP.** You may feel that you'll get into trouble or that something is your fault. Even if you DID mess up, we all make mistakes. You may have got yourself in a tricky or risky situation with someone online. Don't worry. Whatever has happened, it is important to speak up, so that it can get taken care of.

DON'T:

Use your name or email as your username.

Reply to upsetting messages.

Share photos of yourself or other people.

MAKE A PLAN

Cyberbullying is upsetting. Make a plan for something nice you can do away from your screens with someone that would make you feel better if it happens.

I would:

With:

DO:

Keep personal details to yourself.

Stay respectful online.

Block users who upset you or make you feel uncomfortable.

LOSS

When we lose something, we feel sad. That feeling of sadness can be big if we lose a person we love. It's normal to be upset, to cry, and to miss them. Over time, those feelings fade and we feel better, although we may never forget the person.

Make a memory box

It can make us happy to remember good times with the person we've lost. To help remember, why not make a memory box to capture all those good times?

You will need a box with a lid. You can decorate it however you like. Here are some ideas of things you could put in the box:

- Information about their childhood
- Photos of special times you shared
- Their funeral booklet
- Something related to their job
- Things to do with their hobbies, like gardening gloves or a favorite puzzle
- A picture or postcard of their favorite place
- Photos of their childhood
- Things they were proud of
- Things they would say
- Their favorite book, film, sport, or music
- Jewelry or a piece of clothing
- Their favorite perfume or aftershave
- A list of things you miss about them

Good memories

If you have lost someone you loved, some days can be harder than others, like Christmas Day or their birthday. Decide if you want to have special time on those days to talk about the person who has gone and celebrate them. On those days, you could:

Talk about the person who has died.

Write a letter to them.

Eat their favorite food.

Wear their sweater.

Light a candle.

Visit the grave.

Listen to some music.

Cry and laugh as you remember them.

HAPPY HELPING

Experts say that helping others makes us happy. What do you think? Can you remember a time you helped someone else and it made you feel good? Draw a time when you helped someone.

Who did you help?
Was anyone else there?
What did you feel?

There are lots of ways you can help others, at home, at school, or in the wider world. Come up with an idea for something you can do to help others for each of the places.

Where?	Example	My idea
At home	Wash up after dinner.	
At school	Be nice to someone sitting on their own.	
Wider world	Cut down my use of plastic.	

MORE IDEAS

Here are some more ideas. Circle the ones you will do this week! Keep coming back for ideas.

Turn off your phone to listen to someone.

Give someone a compliment.

Leave a kind message for someone to find.

Say thank you to someone who helps you.

Share a happy memory with a friend.

Donate an item to a foodbank.

Pick up litter.

Do something helpful for someone in your family.

Smile today.

Congratulate someone for an achievement.

Call a relative you haven't spoken to for a while.

Do some shopping for an elderly neighbor.

Do you have any more ideas? Write them here.

47